LEARN TO DRAW... OUTER SPACE!

Illustrated by Kerren Barbas Steckler

Designed by Heather Zschock

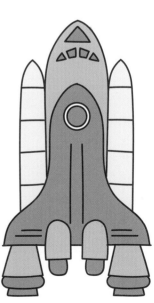

PETER PAUPER PRESS, INC.

White Plains, New York

For Emily and Audrey

Each of you has demonstrated
commitment that is out of this world!
So proud of the both of you!

PETER PAUPER PRESS

In 1928, at the age of twenty-two, Peter Beilenson began
printing books on a small press in the basement of his parents'
home in Larchmont, New York. Peter—and later, his wife,
Edna—sought to create fine books that sold at "prices even a
pauper could afford."

Today, still family owned and operated, Peter Pauper Press
continues to honor our founders' legacy of quality, value, and
fun for big kids and small kids alike.

Illustrations copyright © 2022 Kerren Barbas Steckler
Designed by Heather Zschock

Published in the United Kingdom and Europe by
Peter Pauper Press, Inc. c/o White Pebble International
Units 2-3, Spring Business Park
Stanbridge Road
Havant, Hampshire PO9 2GJ, UK

7 6 5 4 3 2 1

Hey, young artists!

Are you ready to learn how to draw
35 things in outer space?
It's easy and fun!
Just follow these steps:

First, pick an astronaut, rocket, or other picture you want to draw.

Next, trace over the picture with a pencil. This will give you a feel for how to draw the lines.

Then, following the numbers, start drawing each new step (shown in red) of the picture in the empty space in each scene, or on a piece of paper.

Lastly, if you're an awesome artist (and of course, you are!), try drawing a whole scene with one or more astronauts, aliens, rockets, and more. And remember, don't worry if your drawings look different from the ones in this book—outer space is full of possibilities!

You're on your way to creating your own special masterpieces!

GET READY! GET SET! DRAW!

1.

2.

3.

Follow each new step
in red to draw this **alien**.

4.

5.

6.

1.

2.

3.

Follow each new step
in red to draw this **alien**.

4.

5.

6.

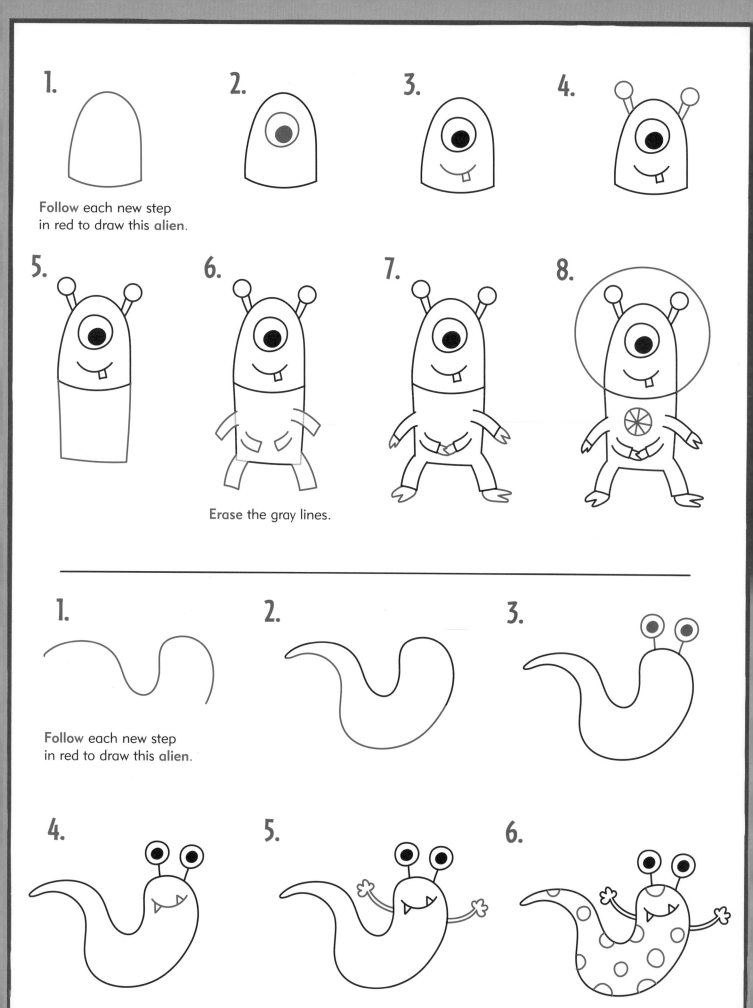

1.

2.

3.

4.

Follow each new step in red to draw this **alien**.

5.

6.

7.

8.

Erase the gray lines.

1.

2.

3.

Follow each new step in red to draw this **alien**.

4.

5.

6.

1.

Follow each new step in red to draw this **alien ship**.

2.

3.

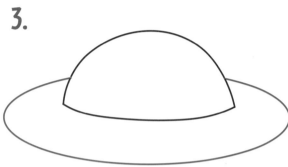

4.

5.

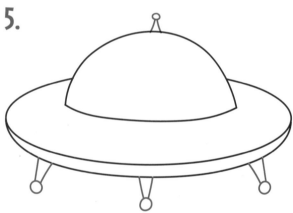

6.

7.

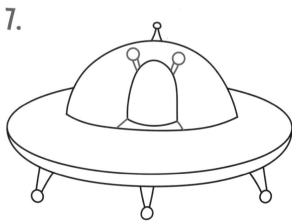

8.

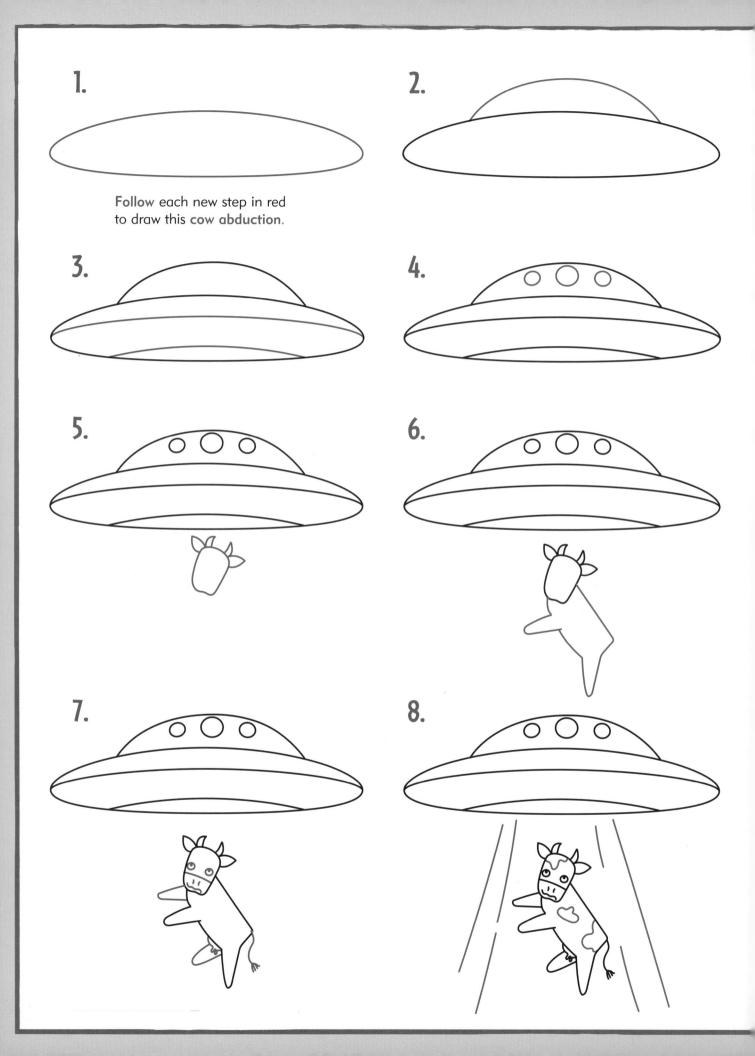

1.

2.

Follow each new step in red
to draw this **cow abduction**.

3.

4.

5.

6.

7.

8.

1.

2.

3.

Follow each new step in red
to draw this **rocket ship**.

4.

5.

6.

Trace over me for practice!

1.

2.

3.

4.

Follow each new step in red to draw this space cat.

5.

6.

7.

8.

9.

10.

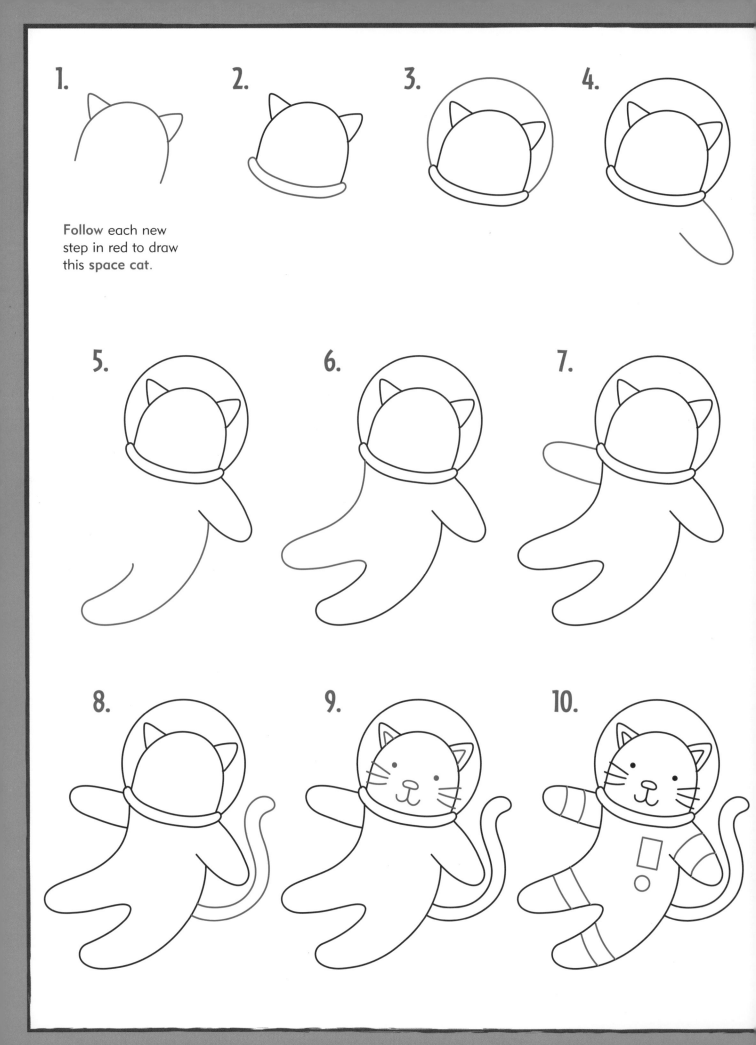

Trace over me
for practice!

1.

Follow each new
step in red to draw
this **space dog**.

2.

3.

4.

5.

6.

7.

8.

9.

10.

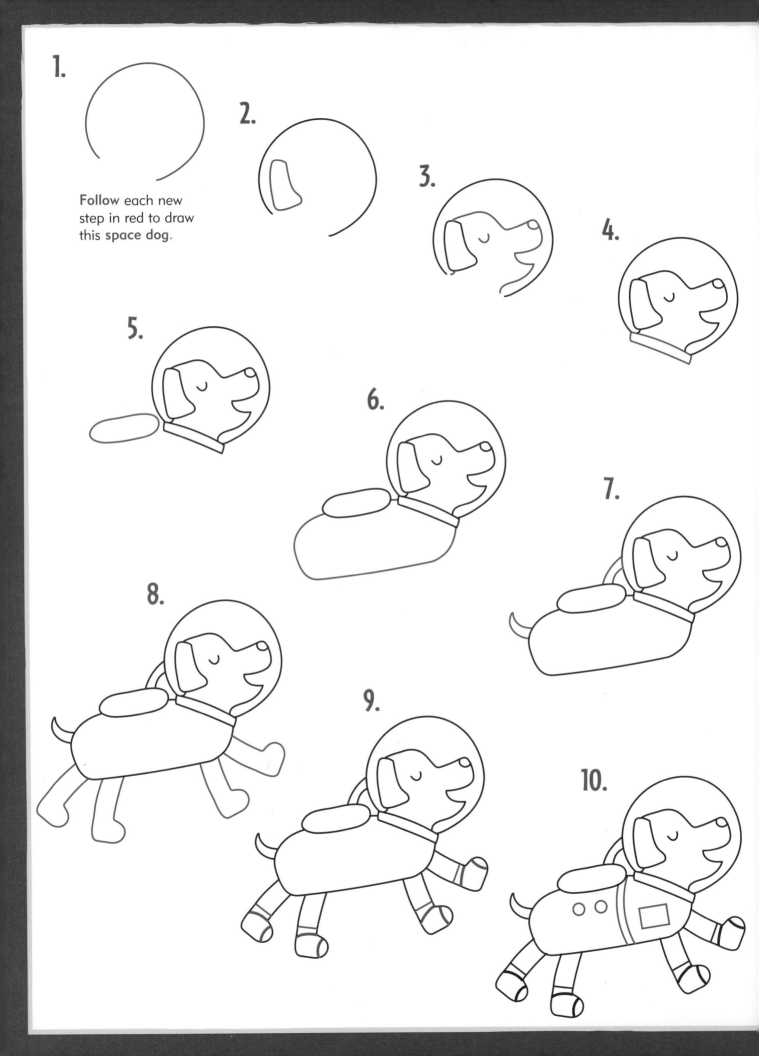

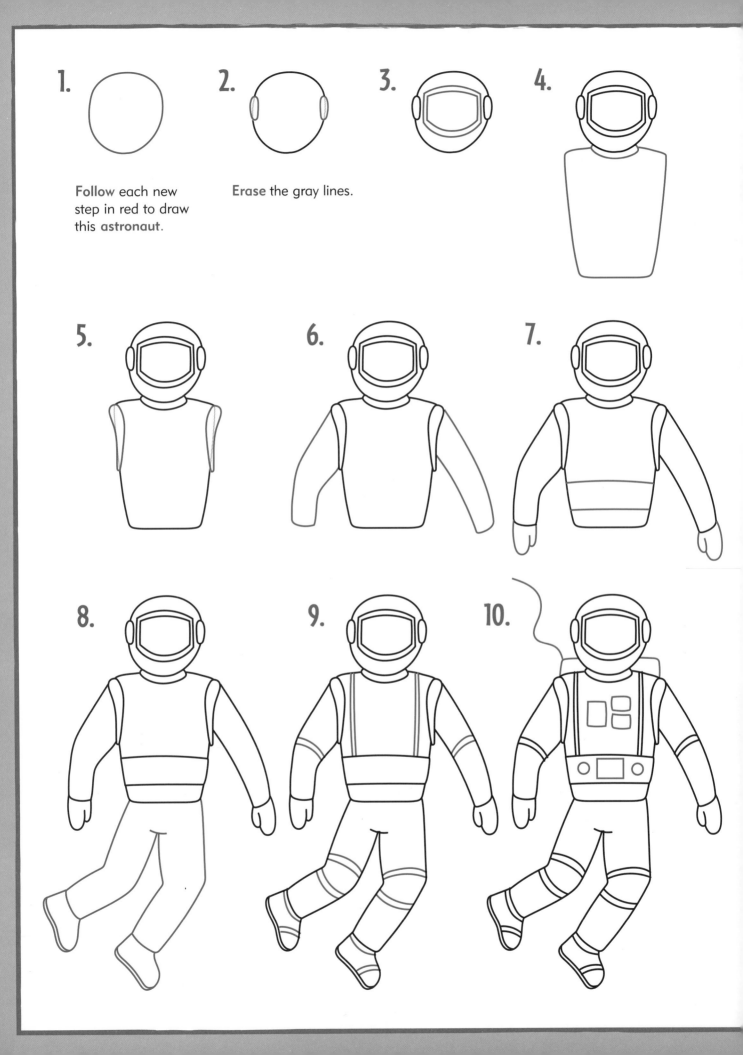

1.

2.

Follow each new
step in red to draw
this **astronaut**.

Erase the gray lines.

3.

4.

5.

6.

7.

8.

9.

10.

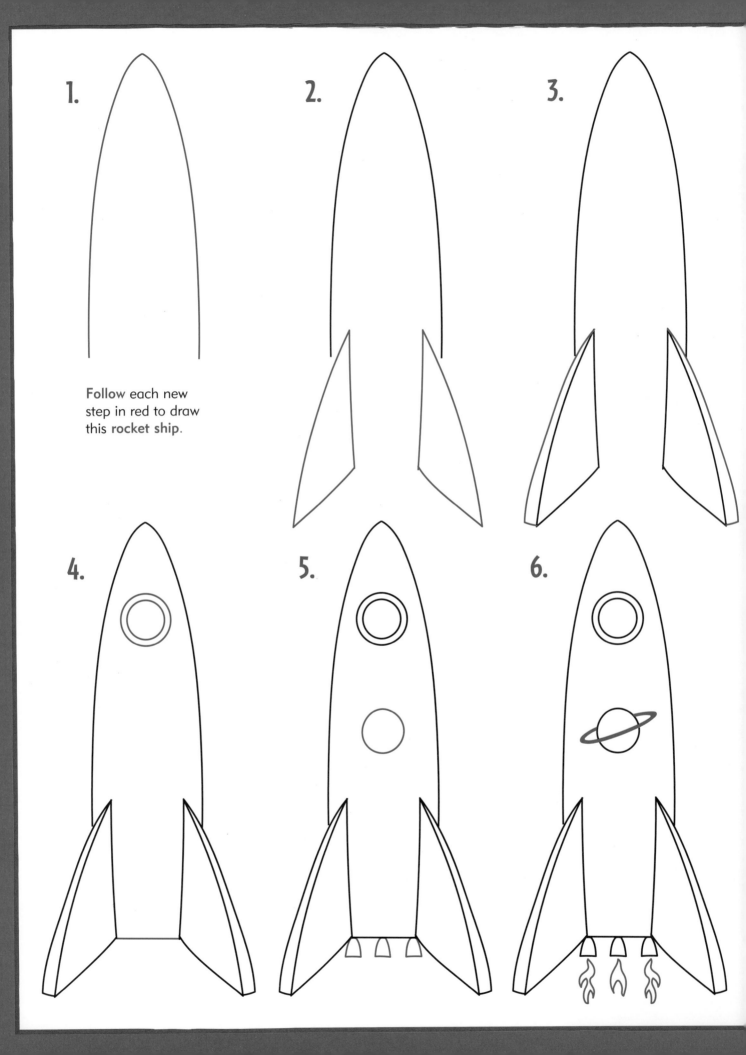

1.

2.

3.

4.

5.

6.

Follow each new step in red to draw this **rocket ship**.

Trace over me
for practice!

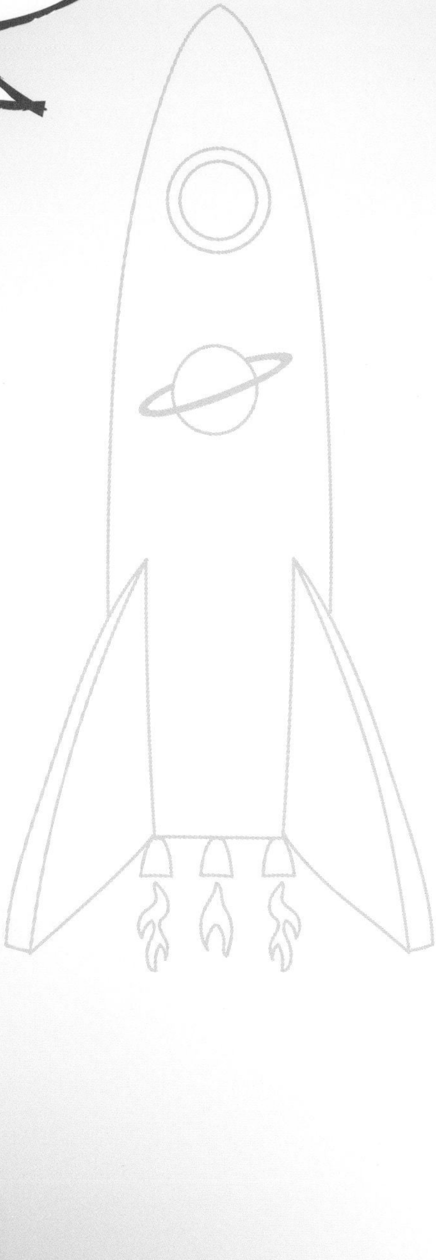

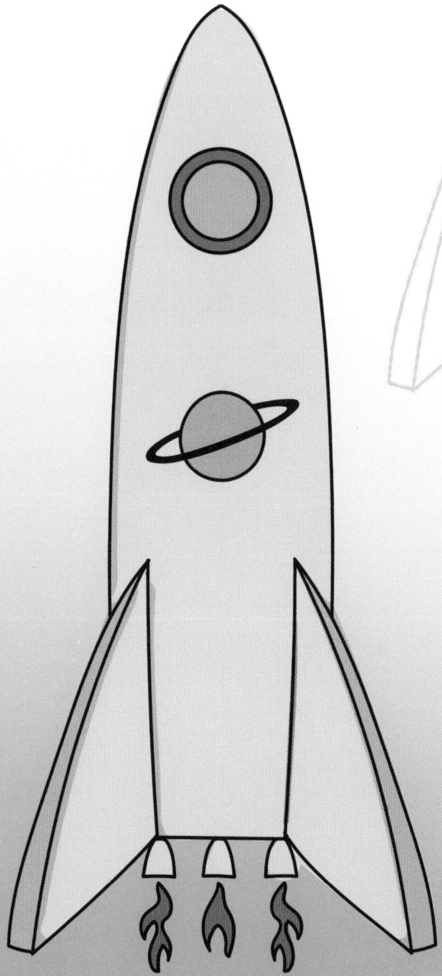

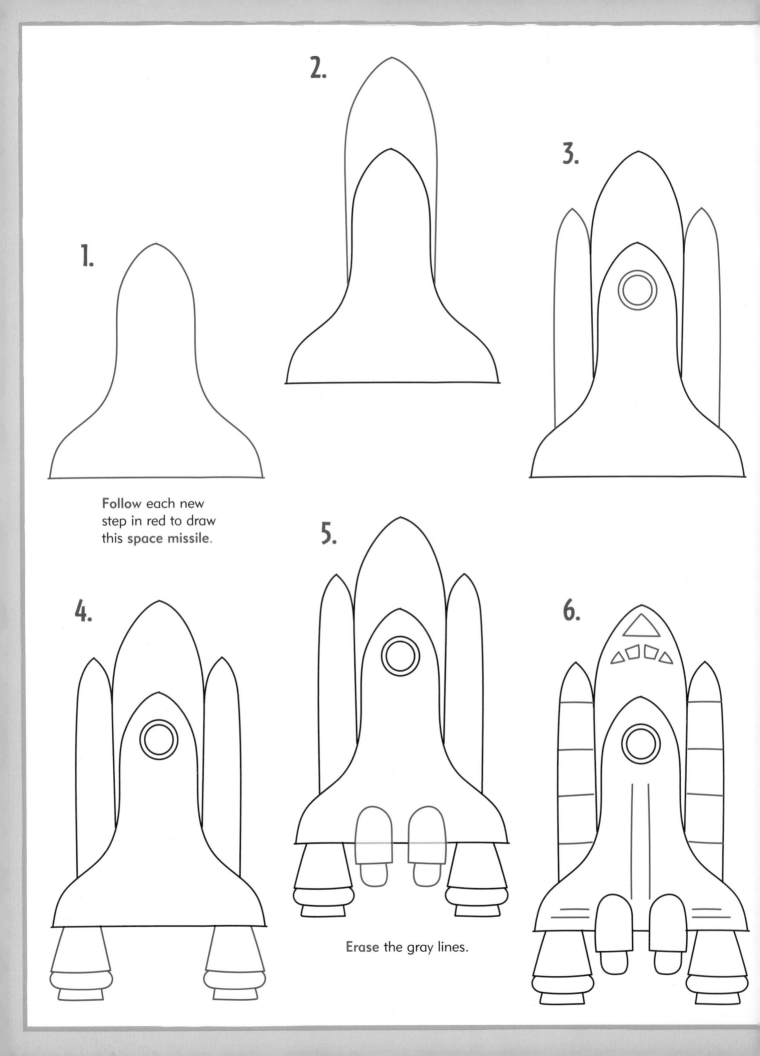

1.

Follow each new step in red to draw this **space missile**.

2.

3.

4.

5.

Erase the gray lines.

6.

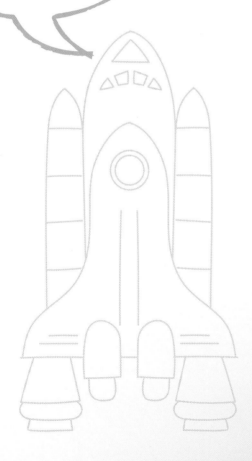

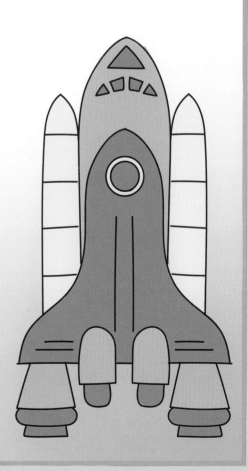

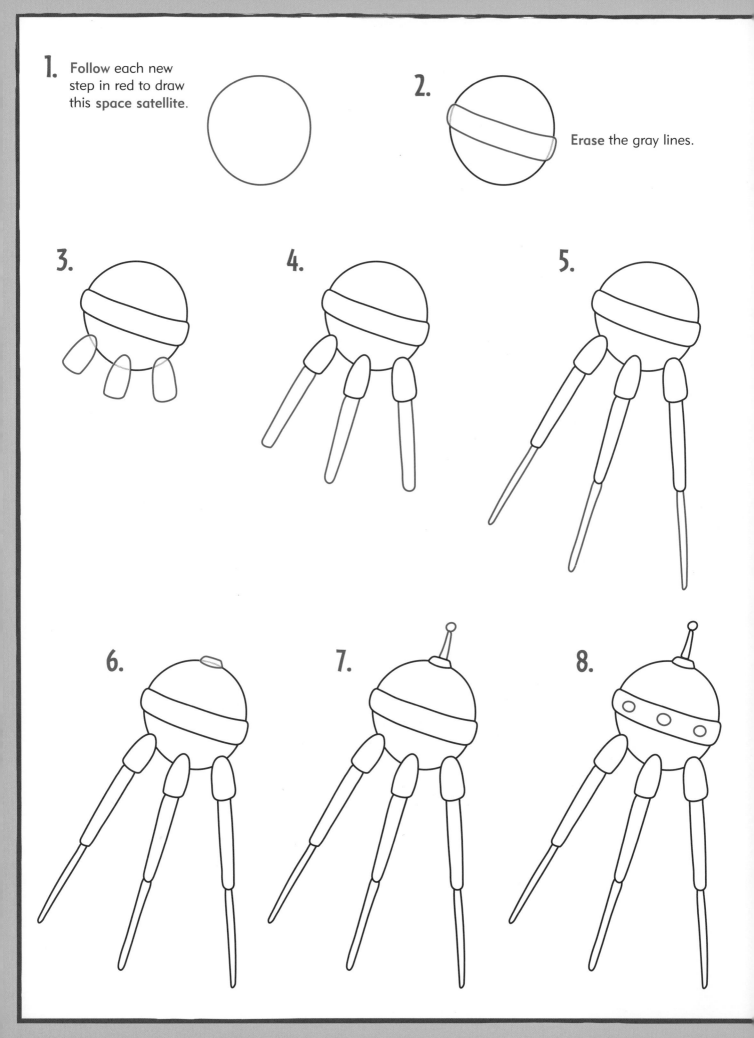

1. Follow each new step in red to draw this **space satellite**.

2. Erase the gray lines.

3.

4.

5.

6.

7.

8.

1.

Follow each new step in red to draw this space probe.

2.

3.

4.

Erase the gray lines.

5.

6.

7.

8.

9.

10.

11.

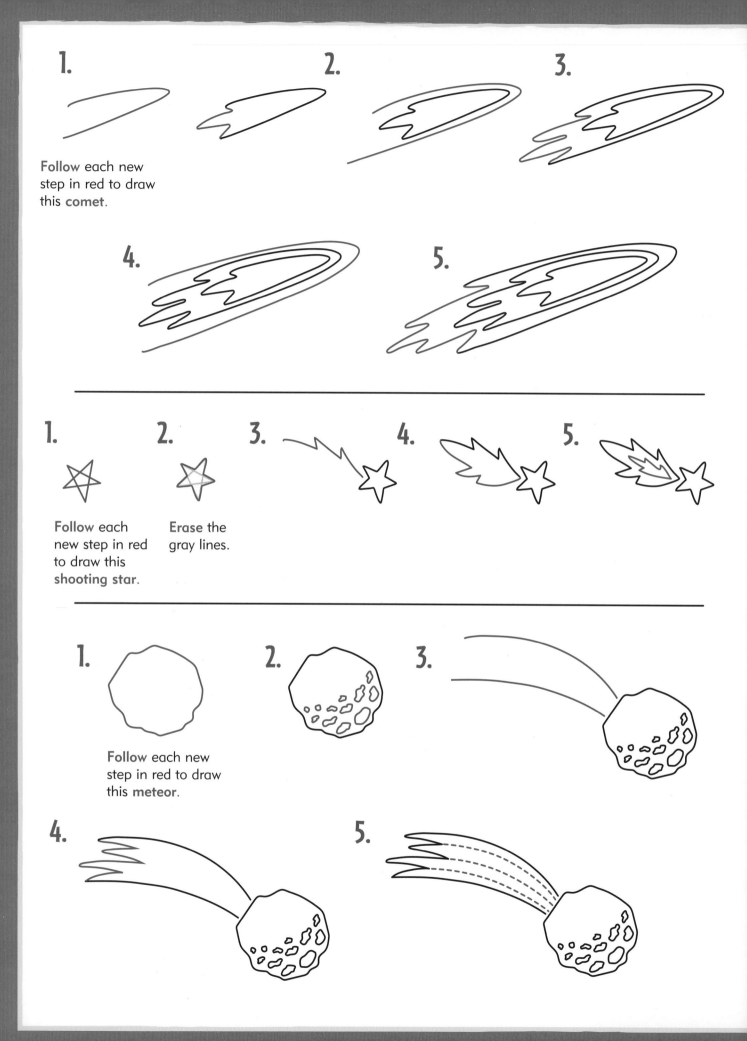

1.

2.

3.

Follow each new step in red to draw this **comet**.

4.

5.

1.

2.

3.

4.

5.

Follow each new step in red to draw this **shooting star**.

Erase the gray lines.

1.

2.

3.

Follow each new step in red to draw this **meteor**.

4.

5.

Trace over us for practice!

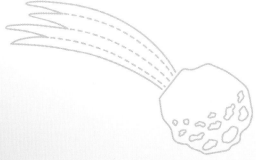

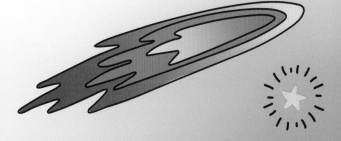

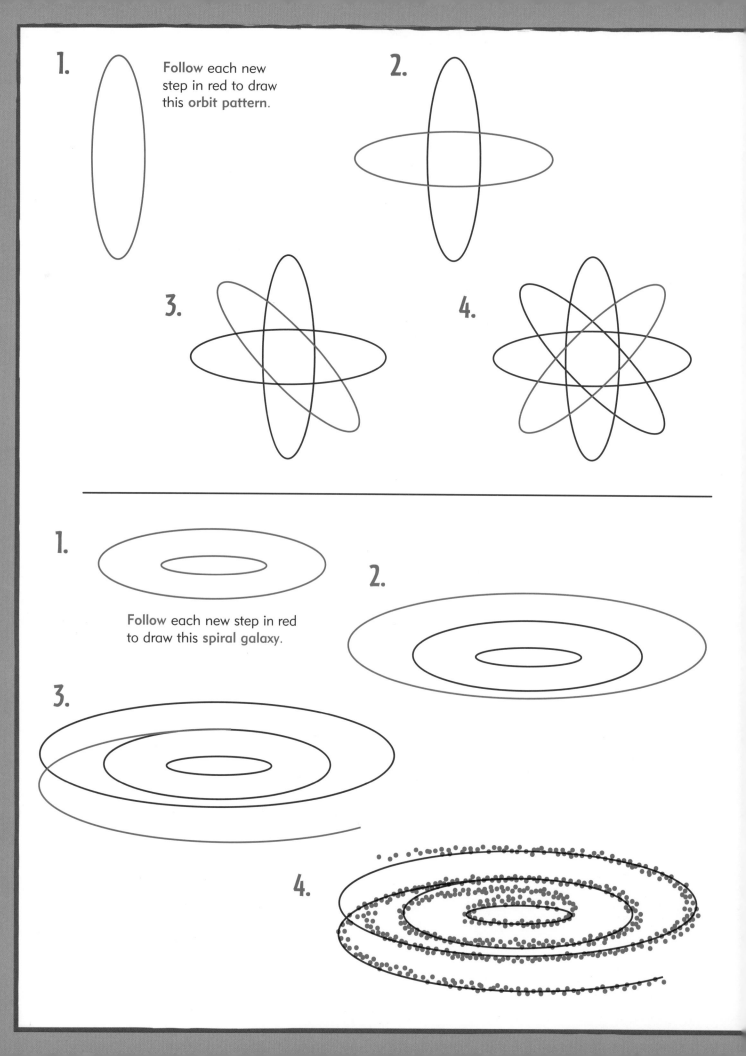

1. Follow each new step in red to draw this **orbit pattern**.

2.

3.

4.

1.

Follow each new step in red to draw this **spiral galaxy**.

2.

3.

4.

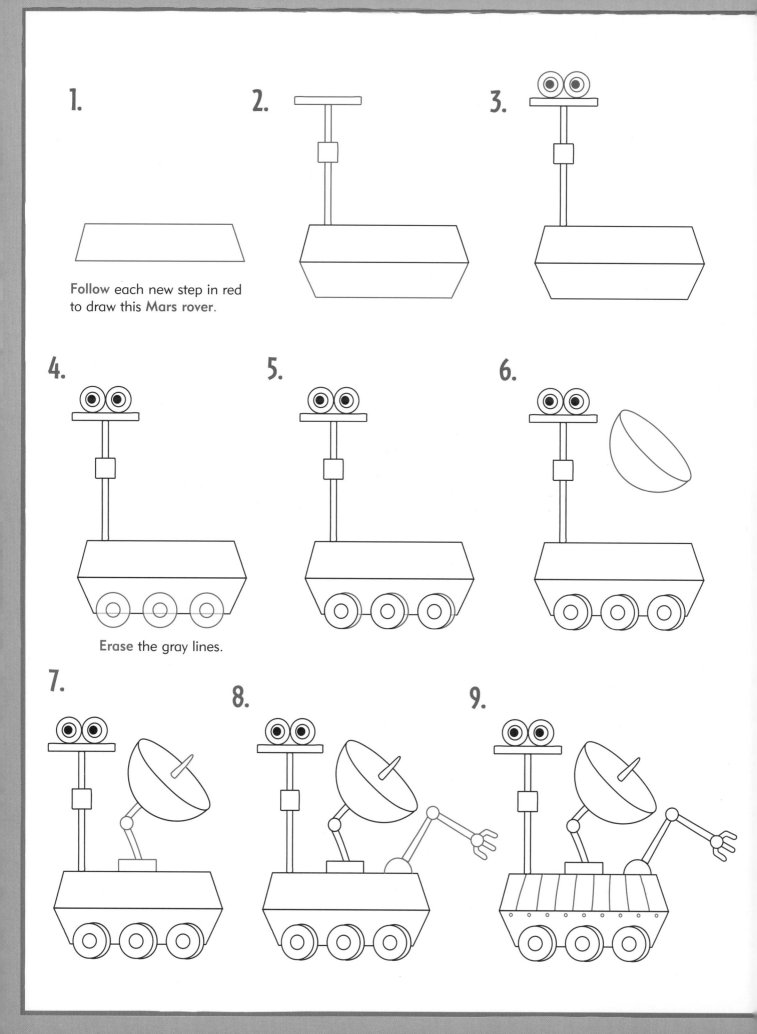

1.

Follow each new step in red to draw this **Mars rover**.

2.

3.

4.

Erase the gray lines.

5.

6.

7.

8.

9.

1.

Follow each new step in red
to draw this **space station**.

2.

3.

4.

5.

Erase the gray lines.

6.

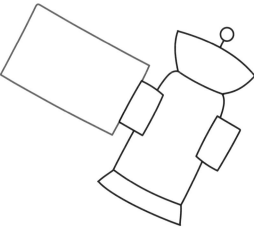

7.

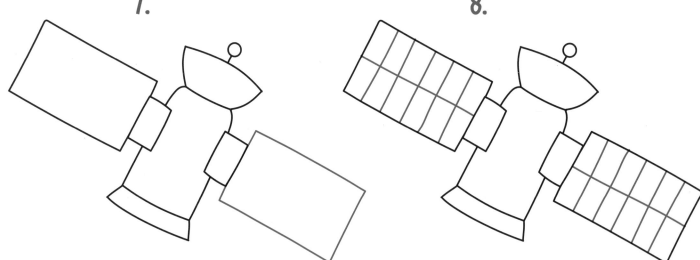

8.

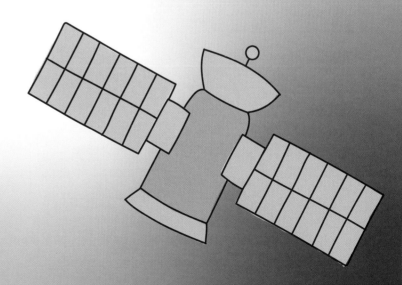

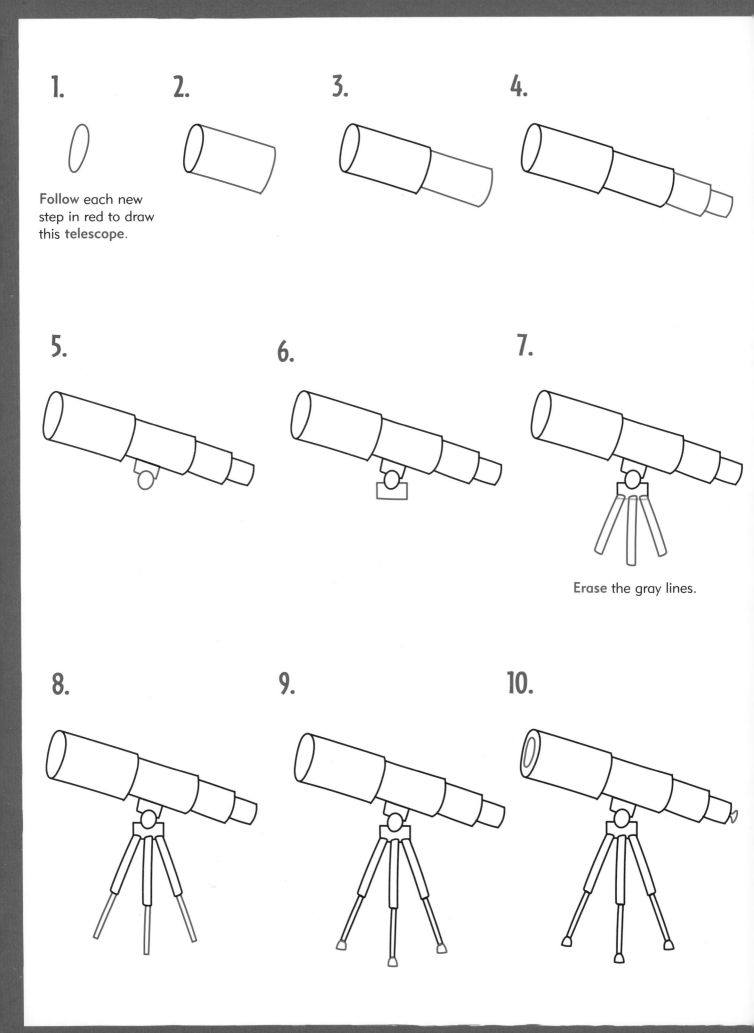

1.

Follow each new
step in red to draw
this **telescope**.

2.

3.

4.

5.

6.

7.

Erase the gray lines.

8.

9.

10.

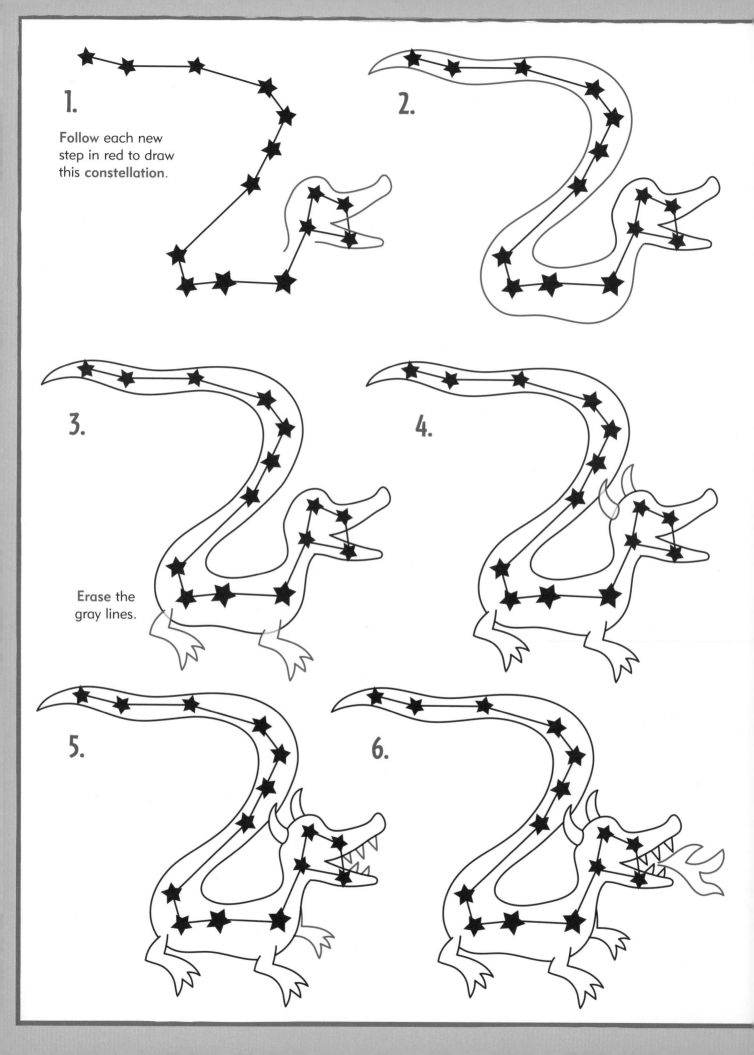

1.

Follow each new step in red to draw this **constellation**.

2.

3.

Erase the gray lines.

4.

5.

6.

1.

Follow each new step in red to draw this **constellation**.

2.

3.

4.

5.

6.

7.

8.

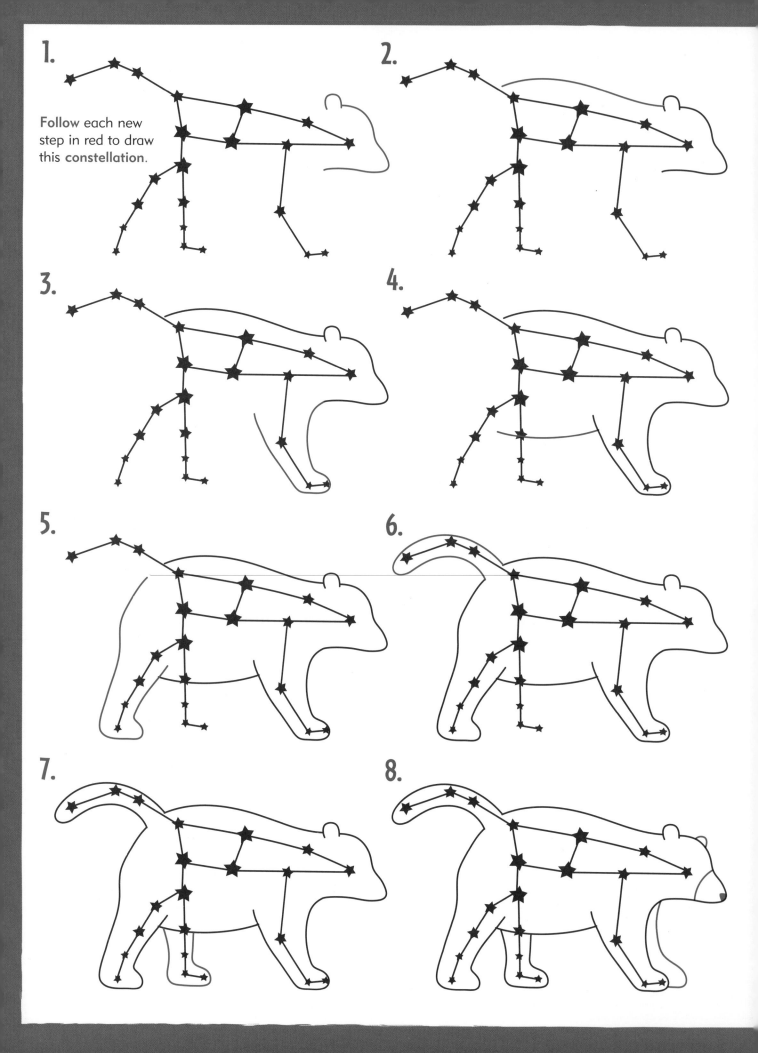

5. MARS

6. JUPITER

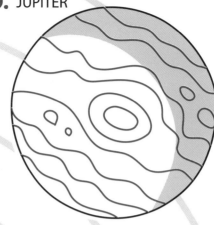

8. URANUS

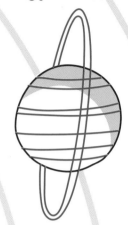

Follow each new step in red to draw this **solar system**.

2. MERCURY

3. VENUS

1. SUN

7. SATURN

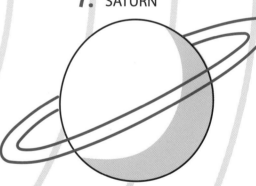

4. EARTH

9. NEPTUNE

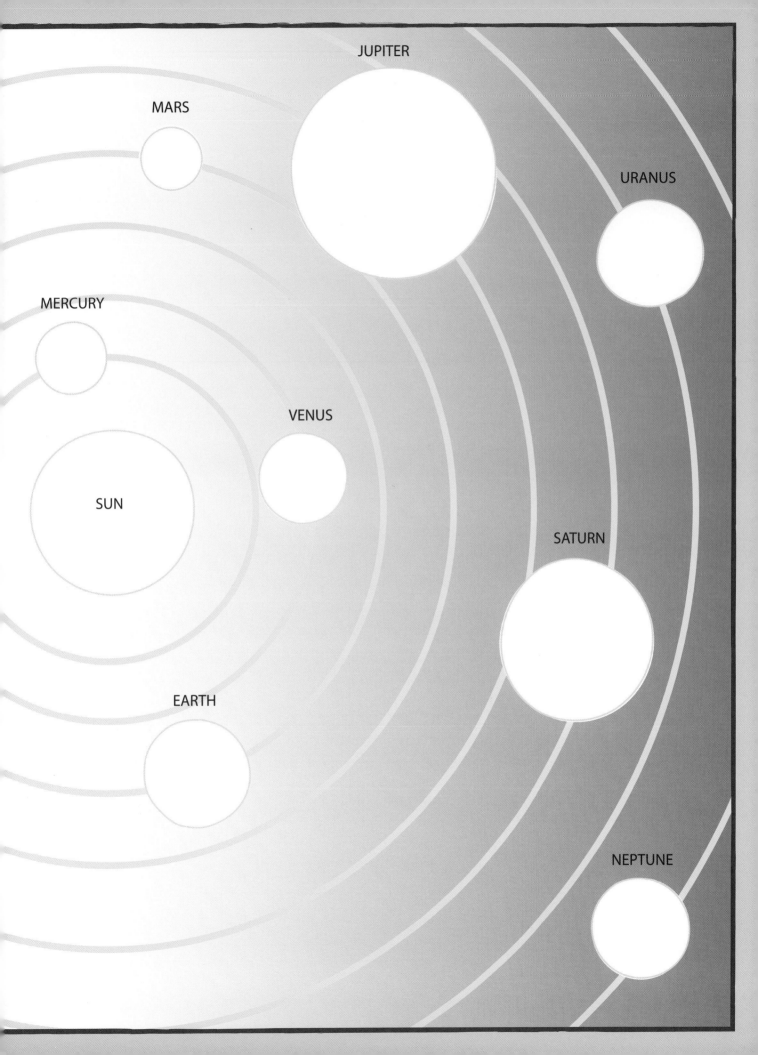

1. Follow each new step in red to draw this planetarium.

2.

3.

Erase the gray lines.

4.

5.

6.

7.

8.

9.

1.

Follow each new step in red to draw this **astronaut**.

2.

Erase the gray lines.

3.

4.

5.

6.

7.

8.

9.

We've reached the end,
and now we're done.
Outer space
is so much fun!